approx	approximately		patt	pattern(s)
beg	begin/beginning		pc	popcorn
bet	between		pm	place marker
BL	back loop(s)		prev	previous
BP	back post		rem	remain/remaining
BPdc	back post double crochet		rep	repeat(s)
CC	contrasting color		rev sc	reverse single crochet
ch	chain(s)		rnd(s)	round(s)
ch-	refers to chain or space previously made, e.g., ch-1 space		RS	right side(s)
			sc	single crochet
ch lp	chain loop		sc2tog	single crochet 2 stitches together
ch-sp	chain space		sk	skip
CL	cluster(s)		Sl st	slip stitch
cm	centimeter(s)		sp(s)	space(s)
cont	continue		st(s)	stitch(es)
dc	double crochet		tbl	through back loop(s)
dc2tog	double crochet 2 stitches together		tch	turning chain
			tfl	through front loop(s)
dec	decrease/decreases/decreasing		tog	together
FL	front loop(s)		tr	triple crochet
foll	follow/follows/following		tr2tog	triple crochet 2 stitches together
FP	front post		trtr	triple treble crochet
FPdc	front post double crochet		WS	wrong side(s)
FPtr	front post triple crochet		yd	yard(s)
g	gram(s)		yo	yarn over
hdc	half double crochet		yoh	yarn over hook
inc	increase/increases/increasing		[]	Work instructions within brackets as many times as directed
lp(s)	loop(s)			
m	meter(s)		*	Repeat instructions following the single asterisk as directed
MC	main color			
mm	millimeter(s)		**	Repeat instructions between asterisks as many times as directed or repeat from a given set of instructions
oz	ounce(s)			
p	picot			

metallic **tunic**

This light-as-a-feather tunic is great for holiday parties or a special occasion. Layer it over a tank or camisole and pair it with a long skirt or pants for an elegant look. The easy stitch pattern creates an open-work fabric that is quick and easy to crochet.

yarn
Lightweight metallic

1X: 1,467 yd (1,350 m)
2X: 1,630 yd (1,500 m)
3X: 1,793 yd (1,650 m)
4X: 1,956 yd (1,800 m)

hooks
6/G (4 mm) for main body
5/F (3.75 mm) for sleeve and neck borders

stitches
Single crochet
Double crochet

gauge
7 V-sts = 4" (10.2 cm) using 6/G hook

notions
Tapestry needle
Button, ½" (1.3 cm) diameter
Hand-sewing needle
Thread

finished size
1X (2X, 3X, 4X)
Bust size 48" (50", 52", 54")
[121.9 (127, 132.1, 137.2) cm]

notes

*1. **To dec V-st,** on first row, work only 1 dc in V, omit ch 2 and second dc. On second row, omit second dc, thereby dec 1 V-st.*

*2. **To inc V-st,** on first row, work extra dc in first st and last st. On second inc row, ch 5 (counts as dc and ch 2), work 1 more dc bet first 2 dc (this creates new V-st), cont across row, create new V between last 2 dc, ending 1 dc.*

back

Foundation row: With 6/G hook, ch 132 (138, 144, 150). Starting in sixth ch from hook (counts as dc), * [1 dc, ch 2, 1 dc] in next ch (V-stitch made), sk 2 ch, rep from * across row, ending 1 dc in last ch, turn—42 (44, 46, 48) V-sts and 1 dc each side.

Row 1: Ch 3 (counts as dc), * [1 dc, ch 2, 1 dc] in next ch-2 sp, rep from * across row, ending with 1 dc in top of tch, turn.

Rep row 1 until piece measures 14½" (15", 15½", 16") [36.8 (38.1, 39.4, 40.6) cm] from beg.

Armhole shaping: Sl st over 4 V-sts, ch 3 (counts as dc), work on center 34 (36, 38, 40) V-sts, turn, leave rem 4 V-sts unworked—34 (36, 38, 40) V-sts and 1 dc each side.

Cont in patt as established, dec 1 st each edge every row 4 times—30 (32, 34, 36) V-sts and 1 dc each side.

Cont in patt as established until armhole measures 9½" (10", 10½", 11") [24.1 (25.4, 26.9, 27.9) cm]. Fasten off.

front

Work same as back until armhole shaping is completed.

Keyhole shaping

Left side: Work across 15 (16, 17, 18) V-sts, work 1 dc in center of next V, turn, leave rem V-sts unworked. Work on 15 (16, 17, 18) V-sts until armhole measures 7" (7½", 8", 8½") [17.8 (19.1, 20.3, 21.6) cm], ending at side edge.

Neck shaping: Ch 3 (counts as dc), work on center across 9 (10, 10, 11) V-sts, turn, leave rem leaving 6 (6, 7, 7) V-sts unworked for neck—9 (10, 10, 11) V-sts and 1 dc each side. Working on rem V-sts, dec 1 (2, 1, 2) V-st at neck edge—8 (8, 9, 9) V-sts and 1 dc each side. Work even until same length as back to shoulder. Fasten off.

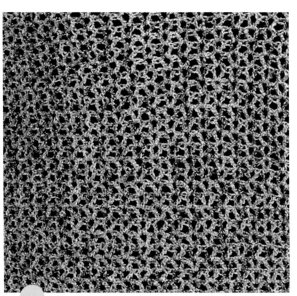

Simple V-stitch pattern is made by working double crochet, chain two, double crochet in a single stitch. In every row, the V-stitch pattern is worked into the chain space of the row before.

Right side: Join yarn in center V same as left front, ch 3, work rem 15 (16, 17, 18) V-sts until 7" (7½", 8", 8½") [17.8 (19.1, 20.3, 21.6) cm, ending at neck edge.

Neck shaping: Sl st over 6 (6, 7, 7) V-sts, ch 3, work rem 9 (10, 10, 11) V-sts.

Working on rem V-sts, dec 1 (2, 1, 2) V-st at neck edge—8 (8, 9, 9) V-sts and 1 dc each side. Work even until same length as back to shoulder. Fasten off.

sleeves
Make 2.

Foundation row: With 5/ F hook, ch 60 (66, 72, 78). Work same as back on 18 (20, 22, 24) V-sts for 4 rows. Change to 6/G hook, inc 1 st each edge every third row 18 times—36 (38, 40, 42) V-sts. Work even until sleeve measures 16" (16½", 17", 17½") [40.6 (41.9, 43.2, 44.5) cm] from beg.

Sleeve cap: Sl st over 4 V-sts, work to last 4 V-sts, turn, leave rem sts unworked—28 (30, 32, 34) V-sts.

Dec 1 st each edge every row 20 times. Fasten off.

finishing
1. Sew shoulder seams.
2. Mark center of sleeve cap, pin center of sleeve to shoulder seam, pin underarms in place, sew in sleeve, easing in to fit.
3. Sew underarm seams.
4. Work neck border.
5. Sew on button.
6. Weave in ends using a tapestry needle.
7. Do not block.

neck border
Row 1: With RS facing and 5/F hook, join yarn at right shoulder seam, work 1 row sc across back neck, working 1 sc in each dc, cont along side and left front of neck, working 3 sc in corner, cont in sc down front opening, up right front to corner, work 1 sc in corner, ch 10 for buttonloop, work another sc in corner, cont along right front neck back to where you started, Sl st in first sc to join.

Row 2: 1 sc in each sc to first corner, work 3 sc in corner, cont down left front to last st on left front, skip this st and first st on right front, cont up right front, working 3 sc in button loop st, cont along right neck edge, Sl st in first sc to join. Fasten off.

A keyhole neckline opening closes with a chain loop around a rhinestone button.

beaded rayon **shell**

Pair this shell with a cardigan, or wear it alone.
It's also great for layering under a suit jacket.
This beaded rayon yarn has rich colors and
a lovely sheen.

yarn
Medium-weight textured

750 yd (960 m)

hooks
6/G (4 mm) for main body
5/F (3.75 mm) for trim

stitches
Single crochet
Double crochet

gauge
15 dc = 4" (10.2 cm) using 6/G
hook

notion
Tapestry needle

finished size
1X (2X, 3X, 4X)
Bust size 45" (47", 49", 51")
[114.3 (119.4, 124.5, 129.5) cm]

notes

When working in dc, dec by dc2tog. Always work dec 1 st in from end sts.

back

Foundation row: With 6/G hook, ch 85 (89, 93, 97). Starting in second ch from hook (counts as sc), 1 sc in each ch across, turn—84 (88, 92, 96) sc.

Row 1: Ch 3 (counts as dc), sk first sc, * 1 dc in next 82 (86, 90, 94), 1 dc in top of tch—84 (88, 92, 96) dc.

Rep row 1 for 2½" (3", 3", 3½") [6.4 (7.6. 7.6, 8.9) cm]. Change to smaller hook and work in dc for 2" (5.1 cm) more. Change back to larger hook and work in dc until piece measures 13" (13½", 14", 14½") [33 (34.3, 35.6, 36.8) cm] from beg.

Armhole shaping: Sl st in 8 sts, ch 3 (counts as dc), 1 dc in next 67 (71, 75, 79) sts, turn, leave rem 8 dc unworked—68 (72, 76, 80) dc.

Cont as established, dec 1 st at each side every row 4 times—60 (64, 68, 72) sts. Work even until armhole measures 9" (9½", 10", 10½") [22.9 (24.1, 25.4, 26.9) cm]. Fasten off.

front

Work same as for back until all armhole dec are completed.

V-neck shaping:

Left side: Work across 30 (32, 34, 36) sts, turn. Leave rem sts unworked. Working on left side only, dec 1 st at neck edge every row 17 (18, 20, 21) times—13 (14, 14, 15) sts. Work even until same length as back to shoulder. Fasten off.

Right side: Join yarn at center with Sl st, work 30 (32, 34, 36) dc across rem sts of row. Working on right side only, work as for left front, reversing shaping.

Rows of double crochet make for quick work. The yarn changes color frequently and creates a random design.

Single crochet border rows are edged with a row of dainty picot stitches.

finishing

1. Sew shoulder seams.
2. Sew underarm seams.
3. Work neck and armhole borders.
4. Weave in ends using a tapestry needle.
5. Block to measurements.

neck border

Rnd 1: With RS facing, join yarn at right shoulder using smaller hook, work 1 sc in each st along back of neck, work in sc evenly spaced along left front down to point of V, cont working sc up right front to shoulder, Sl st in first sc to join. Do not turn.

Rnd 2: Ch 1, 1 sc in each sc until 1 st before point of V, sk last st on left side and first st on right side, 1 sc in each sc to shoulder, Sl st in first sc to join. Do not turn.

Rnd 3 (picot rnd): * Ch 3, work 1 sc in first ch for p, sk 1 st, 1 sc next st, rep from *. Fasten off.

armhole border

Work 3 rnds as for neck border.

color block **tunic**

The bold contrast of black and white splits your figure down the middle and is very flattering. The tunic will span several seasons because it is made in cotton yarn.

yarn
Lightweight cotton

Black:
1X: 1,200 yd (1,096 m)
2X: 1,350 yd (1,233 m)
3X: 1,500 yd (1,307 m)
4X: 1,650 yd (1,507 m)

Cream:
1X and 2X: 1,200 yd (1,096 m)
3X: 1,350 yd (1,233 m)
4X: 1,500 yd (1,307 m)

hooks
8/H (5 mm) for main body
6/G (4 mm) for borders and
sleeve beginning

stitches
Single crochet
Half double crochet
Double crochet
Triple crochet

gauge
6 V-sts = 4" (10.2 cm) using
8/H hook

notion
Tapestry needle

finished size
1X (2X, 3X, 4X)
Bust size 50" (54", 56", 58")
[127 (137.2, 142.2, 147.3) cm]

notes

Backs and fronts are made in 2 pieces and sewn together at the center.

left back

Foundation row: With A and 8/H hook, ch 60 (63, 66, 69). Starting in third ch (counts as hdc), [1 sc, ch 2, 1 sc] in next ch (V-st made), * sk 2 ch, [1 sc, ch 2, 1 sc] in next ch, rep from * across row, ending 1 hdc in last ch—19 (20, 21 22) V-sts and 1 hdc each side.

Row 1 (RS): Ch 2 (counts as hdc), * [1 sc, ch 2, 1 sc] in next ch-2 sp of V-st, rep from * across row, ending 1 hdc in top of tch, turn.

Rep row 1 until piece measures 16" (16½", 17", 17½") [40.6 (41.9, 43.2, 44.5) cm] from beg, ending with WS row.

Armhole shaping: Sl st in 2 V-sts, ch 2 (counts as hdc), work patt as established to end of row, 1 hdc in tch, turn—17 (18, 19, 20) V-sts and 1 hdc each side.

Cont as established until armhole measures 10" (10½", 11", 11½") [25.4 (26.9, 27.9, 29.2) cm]. Fasten off.

right back

Foundation row: With B and 8/H hook, work same as left back to armhole, ending with WS row.

Armhole shaping: Work patt as established in next 17 (18, 19, 20) V-sts, work 1 hdc in sp before next V-st, turn, leave rem sts unworked—17 (18, 19, 20) V-sts and 1 hdc each side.

Cont working same as left back until same length as back to shoulder. Fasten off.

left front

Foundation row: With A and 8/H hook, work same as left back until armhole measures 8" (8½", 9", 9½") [20.3 (21.6, 22.9, 24.1) cm], ending with WS row.

Neck shaping: Work patt as established in first 8 (9, 10, 11) V-sts, work 1 hdc in next sp, turn, leave rem 9 V-sts unworked—8 (9, 10, 11) V-sts and 1 hdc each side.

Work even until piece is same length as back. Fasten off.

V-stitch pattern is created by working a single crochet, chain 2, single crochet into each chain space of the previous row throughout.

right front

Foundation row: With B and 8/H hook, work same as right back until armhole measures 8" (8½", 9", 9½") [20.3 (21.6, 22.9, 24.1) cm], ending with WS row.

Neck shaping: Sl st in first 9 V-sts, ch 2 (counts as hdc), work patt as established on rem 8 (9, 10, 11) V-sts.

Work even until piece is same length as back. Fasten off.

sleeves

Make one in A and one in B.

Foundation row: With 6/G hook, ch 60 (63, 66, 69). Work in patt as for back—19 (20, 21, 22) V-sts and 1 hdc each side. Cont patt as for back for 1" (2.5 cm). Change to 8/H hook and work 1" (2.5 cm) more.

Inc 1 st at each side, then rep inc every fifth row 11 times more—31 (32, 33, 34) V-sts and 1 hdc each side.

Work even until sleeve measures 16" (16½", 17", 18") [40.6 (41.9, 43.2, 45.7) cm]. Fasten off.

finishing

1. Sew center fronts and backs together.
2. Sew shoulder seams.
3. Mark center of sleeve, pin center of sleeve to shoulder seam, pin underarms in place, sew in sleeve, easing in to fit.
4. Sew underarm seams, leaving 5" (12.7 cm) unsewn along each lower side edge for side vents.
5. Work trim.
6. Weave in ends using a tapestry needle.
7. Block to measurements.

bottom, sleeve, and neck trim

Bottom trim: With A and 6/G hook, join yarn at top of right side vent, work sc evenly spaced to lower edge, * [1 hdc, 1 dc, 1 tr, ch 3, work 1 sc in first ch of ch 3, 1 tr, 1 dc, 1 hdc (picot shell completed)] in next V-st, work 1 sc in next V-st, repeat from * across bottom, at next side vent, work sc evenly spaced up one side vent and down other side, repeat from * along bottom edge to first side vent, sc evenly spaced up side vent to first st, Sl st in first st to join. Fasten off.

Sleeve trim: With A and 6/G hook, join yarn at seam, repeat from * of bottom trim all around sleeve edge, Sl st in first st to join. Fasten off.

Neck trim: With A and 6/G hook, join yarn at right shoulder seam, repeat from * of bottom trim all around neck edge, Sl st in first st to join. Fasten off.

lace **pullover**

This loose-fitting pullover with its flattering boat neckline has vertical stripes of lacy stitches separated by ridges. It's comfortable to wear and sure to become a favorite wardrobe item.

yarn
Lightweight wool

1X: 2,123 yd (1,947 m)
2X: 2,316 yd (2,124 m)
3X: 2,509 yd (2,301 m)
4X: 2,702 yd (2,478 m)

hooks
6/G (4 mm) for main body
8/H (5 mm) for border edges

stitches
Double crochet
Front post double crochet
Back post double crochet

gauge
2 repeats of (1 shell and 1 group of FPdc) = 4" (10.2 cm) using 6/G hook

notion
Tapestry needle

finished size
1X (2X, 3X, 4X)
Bust size 48" (52", 56", 60")
[121.9 (132.1, 142.2, 152.4) cm]

note

1. Garment is worked from the top down.

back

Foundation row: With 6/G hook, ch 105 (113, 121, 129). Starting in sixth ch from hook, work [3 dc, ch 2, 3 dc] in same ch, * sk 2 ch, 1 dc in next 3 dc, sk 2 ch, [3 dc, ch 2, 3 dc] next ch, rep from * 11 (12, 13, 14) times more, sk 2 ch, 1 dc last ch, turn—13 (14, 15, 16) shells and 12 (13, 14, 15) groups of 3 dc.

Row 1 (RS): Ch 3, * sk 3 dc, [3 dc, ch 2, 3 dc] in next ch-2 sp (shell made), sk 3 dc, 1 FPdc around each of next 3 dc, rep from * 11 (12, 13, 14) times more, ending sk 3 dc, [3 dc, ch 2, 3 dc] in next ch-2 sp, 1 dc in tch, turn.

Row 2: Ch 3, * shell in center of next shell, 1 BPdc in next 3 dc, rep from * 11 (12, 13, 14) times more, ending shell in last shell, 1 dc in tch, turn.

Rep rows 1 and 2 until piece measures 23" (23½", 24", 24½") [58.4 (59.7, 61, 62.2) cm] from beg. Change to 8/H hook, continue patt as established for 2 more rows. Fasten off.

front

Work same as back.

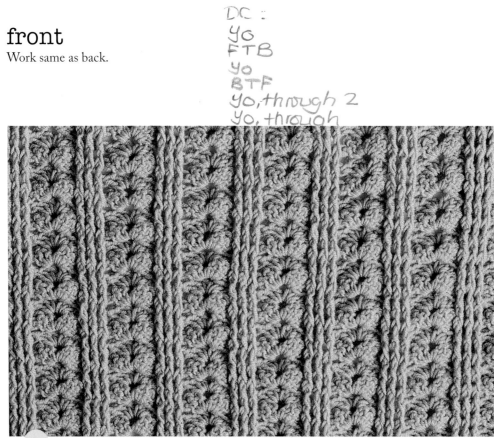

Ridges separating the double crochet shells are created with front post and back post double crochet stitches. The photo shows how they look as you crochet which is upside down from the way they appear in the sweater.

sleeves

Make 2.

Foundation row: With 6/G hook, ch 81 (89, 97, 105). Work same as back on 10 (11, 12, 13) shells until piece measures 11" (12", 13", 14") [27.9 (30.5, 33, 35.6) cm] from beg. Change to 8/H hook, work for 2 more rows. Fasten off.

finishing

1. Sew shoulder seams 7" (7½", 8", 8½") [17.8 (19.1, 20.3, 21.6) cm] in from each side edge.
2. Fold sleeve in half and pin center to shoulder seam. Mark body 8½" (9", 9½", 10") [21.6 (22.9, 24.1, 25.4) cm] down from shoulder, pin ends of sleeves to this marker. Sew sleeve in place.
3. Sew underarm seams.
4. Work neck trim.
5. Weave in ends using a tapestry needle.
6. Do not block.

neck trim

With 6/G hook, join yarn at shoulder seam, starting at right shoulder, working across back of neck, work shell on shell and 3 FPdc on each FPdc, cont along front neck edge, back to beg, Sl st to first st to join. Fasten off.

Because the pullover is worked from the top down, the last rows form a lovely scalloped edge.

The neck is trimmed with a row of shells and ridges worked upward from the foundation row.

short-sleeve **pullover**

The unusual treatment of the hemline of this pullover adds interest with an exciting diagonal line. The shallow V-neckline is finished with a chain-stitch ruffle—very flattering.

yarn
Lightweight cotton

Shown: Grace by Patons, 100% cotton, 1.75 oz (50 g)/136 yd (125 m): Azure #62104, 12 (13, 14, 15) balls

hooks
6/G (4 mm) for main body
5/F (3.75 mm) for trim

stitches
Single crochet
Double crochet

gauge
5 clusters = 4" (10.2 cm) using 6/G hook

notion
Tapestry needle
Pins

finished size
1X (2X, 3X, 4X)
Bust size 49" (53", 56", 59")
[124.5 (134.6, 142.2, 149.9) cm]

notes

1. **Cluster stitch:** *[2 dc, ch 2, 1 sc] in designated st or sp.*
2. **To dec cluster stitch** *at beg of row: Ch 3, eliminating first dc, work [1 dc, ch 2, 1 sc]. On next row, ch 3, eliminate second dc. On third row, eliminate whole CL and go to next CL.*
3. **To dec cluster stitch** *at end of row: Work to last CL, eliminating 1 dc, work [1 dc, ch 2, 1 sc] in last CL, 1 dc in tch. On next row, eliminate second dc, work 1 dc in tch. On third row, eliminate entire CL, ending with 1 dc in tch.*
4. **In order to form "steps"** *when beg this design, it is necessary to ch new sts and form new patts as you work. Be sure you do not twist added ch as you proceed.*

back

Foundation row: With 6/G hook, ch 22 (28, 34, 40). Starting in fourth ch from hook (counts as dc), work [2 dc, ch 2, 1 sc] in next ch, * sk 2 ch, [2 dc, ch 2, 1 sc] in next ch, rep from * 4 (6, 8, 10) times more, ending 1 dc in last ch, turn—6 (8, 10, 12) CL with 1 dc at each edge.

Row 1: Ch 3, * [2 dc, ch 2, 1 sc] in next ch-2 sp, rep from * 5 (7, 9, 11) times more, ending 1 dc in top of tch, turn—6 (8, 10, 12) CL with 1 dc at each edge.

Row 2: Rep row 1, ending with ch 20, turn.

Row 3: Starting in fourth ch from hook (counts as dc), * work [2 dc, ch 2, 1 sc] in next ch, sk 2 ch, rep from * 4 times more across ch, work in patt as established to end of row, 1 dc in top of tch, turn—11 (13, 15, 17) CL with 1 dc at each edge.

Row 4: Ch 3, rep row 1 across row, end with 1 dc top of tch, turn.

Row 5: Rep row 1, turn.

Row 6: Rep row 1, ending with ch 20, turn.

Row 7: Rep row 3, adding 5 new CL across ch-20, then working patt as established across row, 1 dc in top of tch, turn—16 (18, 20, 22) CL with 1 dc at each edge.

Row 8: Rep row 1, turn.

Row 9: Rep row 1, turn.

Row 10: Rep row 1, ending with ch 20, turn.

Clusters of two double crochets, two chains, and a single crochet form each row and are worked into the chain spaces of the row below.

Row 11: Rep row 3, adding 5 new CL across ch-20, then working patt as established across row, 1 dc in top of tch, turn—21 (23, 25, 27) CL with 1 dc at each edge.

Row 12: Rep row 1, turn.

Row 13: Rep row 1, turn.

Row 14: Rep row 1, ending with ch 20, turn.

Row 15: Rep row 3, adding 5 new CL across ch-20, then working patt as established across row, 1 dc in top of tch, turn—26 (28, 30, 32) CL with 1 dc at each edge.

Row 16: Rep row 1, turn.

Row 17: Rep row 1, turn.

Row 18: Rep row 1, ending with ch 20, turn.

Row 19: Rep row 3, adding 5 new CL across ch-20, then working patt as established across row, 1 dc in top of tch, turn—31 (33, 35, 37) CL with 1 dc at each edge.

Cont patt as established on 31 (33, 35, 37 CL until piece measures 16" (16½", 17", 17½") [40.6 (41.9, 43.2, 44.5) cm] from beg.

Armhole shaping: Sl st in first 2 CL, ch 3, cont patt as established in next 27 (29, 31, 33) CL, work 1 dc in sp bet last CL just worked and next CL to form new tch, turn, leave rem sts unworked.

First dec row: Dec 1 dc in first CL, cont across row, dec 1 st in last CL, turn.

Second dec row: Ch 3, omit first partial CL, work as established to last partial CL, sk last CL, ending with dc in top of tch—25 (27, 29, 31) CL with 1 dc at each edge.

Work in patt as established until armhole measures 9½" (10", 10½", 11") [24.1 (25.4, 26.9, 27.9) cm]. Fasten off.

front
Same as back until armhole measures 2½" (3", 3½", 4") [6.4 (7.6, 8.9, 10.2) cm].

Divide for neck:
Left side: Work across 12 (13, 14, 15) CL, work dc bet last CL worked and next CL to form new tch, turn, leave rem 13 (14, 15, 16) CL unworked.

Cont working in patt as established on 12 (13, 14, 15) CL until armhole measures 7" (7½", 8", 8½") [17.8 (19.1, 20.3, 21.6) cm], ending with WS row.

Neck shaping: Work across 8 (8, 9, 9) CL, work 1 dc bet last CL made and next CL to form new tch, turn, leave rem 4 (5, 5, 6) CL unworked.

Working on 8 (8, 9, 9) CL, dec 1 st at neck edge every row 4 times—6 (6, 7, 7) CL rem. Work even until same length as back to shoulder. Fasten off.

Right side: Sk center CL, join yarn in next CL, ch 3, work patt on rem 12 (13, 14, 14) CL, turn.

Keeping patt as established, work on 12 (13, 14, 15) CL until armhole measures 7" (7½", 8", 8½") [17.8 (19.1, 20.3, 21.6) cm], ending with WS row.

Neck shaping: Sl st in first 4 (5, 5, 6) CL, ch 3, work patt on rem 8 (8, 9, 9) CL, turn.

Working on 8 (8, 9, 9) CL, dec 1 st at neck edge every row 4 times—6 (6, 7, 7) CL rem. Work even until same length as back to shoulder. Fasten off.

sleeves
Make 2.

Foundation row: Using 5/F hook, ch 73 (79, 85, 91). Starting in second ch from hook, 1 sc in each ch, turn—72 (78, 84, 90) sc.

Row 1: Ch 1 (counts as sc), sk first sc, 1 sc in each sc across row, turn.

Row 2: Rep row 1, turn.

Begin patt:
Row 1: Change to 6/G hook. Ch 3 (counts as dc), sk 2 sc, * [2 dc, ch 2, 1 sc] in next sc, sk 2 sc, rep from * 22 (24, 26, 28) times more, end with 1 dc in top of tch, turn—23 (25, 27, 29) CL with 1 dc at each edge.

Row 2: Ch 3, * [2 dc, ch 2, 1 sc] in ch-2 space of next CL, rep from * 22 (24, 26, 28) times more, ending with 1 dc in top of tch, turn.

Rep rows 1 and 2 until sleeve measures 6" (6½", 7", 7½") [15.2 (16.5, 17.8, 19.1) cm] from beg.

Sleeve cap: Sl st in first 2 CL, ch 3, cont patt in next 19 (21, 23, 25) CL, work 1 dc bet last CL worked and next CL, turn, leave rem 2 CL unworked.

Work 2 rows even.

Dec 1 st each edge every row until 7 CL remain. Fasten off.

Picot edging trims the neckline and sleeve ends.

finishing

1. Sew shoulder seams, making sure that long and short sides of body match.
2. Mark center of sleeve cap, pin center of sleeve to shoulder seam, pin underarms in place, sew in sleeve, easing in to fit.
3. Sew underarm seams.
4. Work neck and sleeve borders.
5. Weave in ends using a tapestry needle.
6. Block to measurements.

neck border

Row 1: With 5/F hook, starting at bottom right side of neck opening, work 1 row sc evenly spaced up right front, work 3 sc in last st for corner, cont around neck, along back to top of left front, work 3 sc in last st for corner, cont down left front to bottom of neck opening, turn.

Row 2: Ch 1, sk first st, work 1 sc in each sc, working 3 sc in center st of each corner, turn.

Row 3: 1 sc in first st, * ch 5, 1 sc in next st, rep from * around neck opening until last 1½" (3.8 cm) of lower left front, fasten off.

Place right front edging over left front edging and sew in place to form placket. Sew bottom of placket in space between left and right fronts.

sleeve border

With 5/F hook, join yarn at underarm seam, * ch 5, 1 sc in next st, rep from * around bottom of sleeve, fasten off. Rep for other sleeve.

bow tie **pullover**

This garment requires minimal shaping and finishing. While the stitch is unusual, it is not too difficult to master, and the pattern creates flattering vertical lines.

yarn
Lightweight acrylic

Shown: Astra by Patons, 100% acrylic, 1.75 oz (50 g)/133 yd (122 m): Fantasy #08333, 11 (12, 13, 14) balls

hooks
8/H (5 mm) for main body
6/G (4 mm) for trim

stitch
Single crochet

gauge
12 sc = 4" (10.2 cm) using 8/H hook

notion
Tapestry needle

finished size
1X (2X, 3X, 4X)
Bust size 49" (52", 54", 56")
[124.5 (132.1, 137.2, 142.2) cm]

notes

The bow ties are made by creating chains of 7 sts on 3 rows, then gathering center of chains with 1 sc over all 3 chains on fourth row.

back

Foundation row: With 8/H hook, ch 75 (79, 83, 87). Starting in second ch from hook, work 1 sc in each ch across row, turn—74 (78, 82, 86) sc.

Row 1 (RS): Ch 1, sk first sc, 1 sc in next 72 (76, 80, 84) sc, 1 sc in tch, turn.

Row 2: Rep row 1.

Bow tie pattern:
Row 1: Ch 1, sk first sc, 1 sc in next 13 (15, 17, 19) sc, * ch 7, sk next 7 sc, 1 sc in next 6 sc, rep from * twice more, ch 7, sk 7 sc, 1 sc in next 13 (15, 17, 19) sc, 1 sc in top of tch, turn.

Row 2: Ch 1, sk first sc, 1 sc in next 13 (15, 17, 19) sc, * ch 7, sk ch-7 lp, 1 sc in next 6 sc, rep from * twice more, ch 7, sk ch-7 lp, 1 sc in next 13 (15, 17, 19) sc, 1 sc in top of tch, turn.

Row 3: Rep patt row 2.

Row 4: Ch 1, sk first sc, 1 sc in next 13 (15, 17, 19) sc, * ch 3, 1 sc over all 3 bars created by ch-7 lps, ch 3 (bow tie made), 1 sc in next 6 sc, rep from * twice more, ending last rep 1 sc in next 13 (15, 17, 19) sc, 1 sc in top of tch, turn.

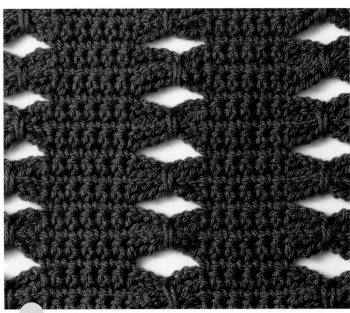

A single crochet stitch encases the loose chains made in the three previous rows to create the bow tie look.

Row 5: Ch 1, sk first sc, 1 sc in next 13 (15, 17, 19) sc, * ch 7, sk bow tie, 1 sc in next 6 sc, rep from * twice more, ch 7, sk bow tie, ending last rep 1 sc in next 13 (15, 17, 19) sc, 1 sc in top of tch, turn.

Rep patt rows 2–5 until piece measures 15½" (16", 16½", 17") [39.4 (40.6, 41.9, 43.2) cm] from beg.

Armhole shaping: Sl st in 7 sts, keep patt as established to last 7 sts, turn, leave rem 7 sts unworked.

Cont patt until armhole measures 8½" (9", 9½", 10") [21.6 (22.9, 24.1, 25.4) cm], ending with row 4.

Shape left side of neck: Ch 1, sk first sc, 1 sc in next 6 (8, 10, 12) sc, ch 7, sk bow tie, 1 sc in next 3 sc, turn, leave rem sts unworked.

Next row: Ch 1, sk first sc, 1 sc in next 2 sc, ch 7, sk ch-7 lp, 1 sc in next 6 (8, 10, 12) sc, 1 sc in top of tch, turn.

Cont patt as established on these sts until 1 bow tie patt is completed, ending with row 4. Fasten off.

Shape right side of neck: Sk center sts, join yarn in third st before last bow tie, ch 1, 1 sc in next 3 sc, ch 7, sk bow tie, 1 sc in next 6 (8, 10, 12) sc, 1 sc in top of tch, turn. Complete as for left side of neck.

front
Work same as back.

sleeves
Make 2.

Foundation row: With 6/G hook, ch 46. Work border as back.

Bow tie pattern:
Row 1: Working with 6/G hook for sizes 1X and 2X and 8/H hook for sizes 3X and 4X, ch 1, sk first sc, 1 sc in next 5 sc, * ch 7, sk next 7 sc, 1 sc in next 6 sc, rep from * twice more, 1 sc in top of tch, turn.

Row 2: Ch 1, sk first sc, 1 sc in next 5 sc, * ch 7, sk ch-7 lp, 1 sc in next 6 sc, rep from * twice more, 1 sc in top of tch, turn.

Row 3: Rep patt row 2.

Row 4: Ch 1, sk first sc, 1 sc in next 5 sc * ch 3, 1 sc over all 3 bars created by ch-7 lps, ch 3 (bow tie made), 1 sc in next 6 sc, rep from * twice more, 1 sc in top of tch, turn.

Row 5: Ch 1, sk first sc, 1 sc in next 5 sc, * ch 7, sk bow tie, 1 sc in next 6 sc, rep from * twice more, 1 sc in top of tch, turn.

Rep patt rows 2–5 once. Change to 8/H hook for all sizes and cont patt, inc 1 st each edge. Then rep inc each edge every fifth row 8 (9, 10, 11) times more (inc sts will be kept in sc). Work even in patt as established until sleeve measures 18" (19", 20", 21") [45.7 (48.3, 50.8, 53.3) cm] from beg, ending with row 4.

Next row: Ch 1, sk first sc, 1 sc in each sc and each ch across row, fasten off.

finishing
1. Sew shoulder seams.
2. Mark center of sleeve top, pin center of sleeve to shoulder seam, pin underarms in place, sew in sleeve.
3. Sew underarm seams.
4. Work neck and sleeve ruffles.
5. Weave in ends using a tapestry needle.
6. Block to measurements.

neck and sleeve ruffles
Neck ruffle: With RS facing, join yarn with Sl st at right shoulder, 1 sc, * ch 5, 1 sc in next st, rep from * around neck edge, Sl st to first sc to join.

Sleeve ruffle: Join yarn with Sl st at seam. Work same as neck ruffle.

A chain-stitch picot edging ruffles softly at the neckline and sleeve ends.

personalizing the fit

Do not be afraid to make adjustments in the length of a garment. Take a moment to measure yourself, and find your size on the chart below. The measurements given in the project specs are the finished measurements of the garment—not your body measurements—so allow for wearing ease.

Measurements	1X	2X	3X	4X
Bust	44" to 46" (111.8 to 116.8 cm)	48" to 50" (121.9 to 127 cm)	52" to 54" (132 to 137.2 cm)	56" to 58" (142.2 to 147.3 cm)
Center back	31" to 31½" (78.7 to 80 cm)	31½" to 32" (80 to 81.3 cm)	32½" to 33" (82.6 to 83.8 cm)	32½" to 33" (82.6 to 83.8 cm)
Back waist length	17¾" (45.1 cm)	18" (45.7 cm)	18" (45.7 cm)	18½" (47 cm)
Cross back (shoulder to shoulder)	17½" (44.5 cm)	18" (45.7 cm)	18" (45.7 cm)	18½" (47 cm)
Sleeve length to underarm	17½" (44.5 cm)	18" (45.7 cm)	18" (45.7 cm)	18½" (47 cm)

For more technique instructions and projects look for *Plus-Size Crochet.*

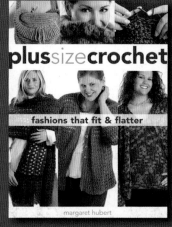

PLUS-SIZE CROCHET
978-1-58923-339-3

This material originally appeared in the book *Plus-Size Crochet* (978-1-58923-339-3) by Margaret Hubert.

$12.99 US / £7.99 UK / $14.99 CAN

Printed in China
ISBN: 978-1-58923-768-1

0 52944 01939 6

9 781589 237681

51299